Tribb's Troubles

)LE

Tribb's Troubles

Grass Roots Press

First published in 2012 by Grass Roots Press

Grass Roots Press gratefully acknowledges the financial support for its publishing programs provided by the following agencies: the Government of Canada through the Canada Book Fund and the Government of Alberta through the Alberta Foundation for the Arts.

Grass Roots Press would also like to thank ABC Life Literacy Canada for their support. Good Reads® is used under licence from ABC Life Literacy Canada.

Library and Archives Canada Cataloguing in Publication

Cole, Trevor, 1960–
   Tribb's troubles / Trevor Cole.

(Good reads series)
ISBN 978–1–926583–84–6

   1. Readers for new literates. I. Title. II. Series: Good reads series (Edmonton, Alta.)

PS8605.O44T75 2012   428.6'2   C2012–902407–4

Printed and bound in Canada.

For K.

Chapter One

Tribb Munday was watching football in his living room. Suddenly, something made him look toward the hall.

Nothing. The hall was empty.

Tribb's wife, Linda, was sitting on the couch against the wall, knitting. Linda worked as a nurse at the local hospital. Lately, whenever she was home, she was knitting.

"Did you see that?" Tribb asked her.

Linda didn't look up. "Was it a good play?" she said.

Tribb shook his head. "I'm not talking about the football game. I thought I saw something in the hall."

In the light coming from the kitchen, Tribb saw the hall carpet and the wall. On the wall hung a framed picture of the Munday family. Tribb, Linda, and Suzy, their daughter. They were standing on the dock of the cottage they'd rented a few summers before. Suzy was eight years old then. That summer, Tribb often thought, was his family's happiest time. But besides the wall, the carpet, and the picture, there was nothing to be seen. Still, Tribb couldn't shake the idea that something else had been there a moment ago. If only he'd looked a second earlier, he'd have seen it.

"I'm sorry, honey," Linda replied. "I'm not really watching the football."

Linda was still focused on her knitting. Every fall she made scarves and mittens and hats to raise money for Suzy's school. This year's sale was at the end of next week, and she had a lot of items to finish. Right now she was working on a powder blue scarf, her long knitting needles clicking in a steady rhythm. Tribb could tell she was not paying any attention to him.

"Linda, it's hard to talk to you when you're not looking at me."

Linda kept knitting. "Okay, then," she said, nodding.

Tribb watched her. "Linda?" he said, and waited. Nothing. "Linda?" he tried again. "Linda? Linda? Linda?"

His wife dropped her hands and the blue scarf into her lap and stared at Tribb with wide eyes. "Tribb, *why* are you *bothering* me? I have all this knitting to do!"

They just looked at each other for a moment.

"Never mind," said Tribb. On the small table beside him sat an old crystal candy dish, a real antique. It held wrapped butterscotch candies, and Tribb tipped the dish to take a few. When he took his hand away, the dish rattled back into place.

"Careful," said Linda. "That dish was my grandmother's. You know it's very precious to me."

Linda paid more attention to the rattle of a dish than to Tribb's own words. He wasn't surprised. That was marriage for you.

"This is looking nice, don't you think?" said Linda.

Out of the corner of his eye, Tribb saw Linda hold up the blue scarf for him to praise. He didn't have to look. He had very good eyesight out of the corner of his eye. Better than most, he thought. Not that anyone else appreciated it.

"Very nice," said Tribb, as he shoved a candy in his mouth.

Chapter Two

Early the next morning, the three Mundays gathered in their bright kitchen. Outside, orange and yellow leaves from two big maple trees covered the yard. At the stove, Linda cooked sausages for breakfast. Tribb and Suzy sat at the kitchen table, holding their thumbs side by side to see whose thumb was longer.

Being eleven years old, Suzy never stopped noticing how her body compared to the bodies of others. Her height, her weight. The number of freckles she had. The thickness of her wrists. The lengths of her fingers and toes. A day did not go by, it seemed, without Suzy judging some part of her body against someone else's. Tribb supposed that she kept measuring herself to see how she fit in the world. Like anyone, he thought.

"Your thumb is huge!" Suzy said. She had a playful grin. "It's so big it's gross!"

Tribb waggled his thumb. "It's not gross," he said. "It's impressive."

"It's like the thumb of a monster!" She pretended to be scared and hid behind her hands. Tribb felt pretty sure she'd be an actress when she grew up. Either an actress or a comedian.

"Now, now, Suzy," said Linda at the stove. "You might hurt your father's feelings."

But Tribb smiled. "The Mundays have always had big hands," he said to Suzy. "You should have seen your great-grandfather's."

"Well, I'm a Munday," said Suzy, "and I have a small thumb. A dainty thumb."

"Who wants toast?" Linda asked.

"I do!" said Tribb.

"I do!" said Suzy.

Tribb saw Linda reach for the bread bag on the counter. She opened it and pulled out a handful of bread slices. She was about to drop two into the toaster when she paused. She looked at the slices.

"Someone's taken a bite out of these pieces of bread." She looked at Tribb. "Who would do that?"

"Not me!" said Tribb. He looked at Suzy. Suzy had made her thumb and index finger into a circle. She held the circle over her fork and squinted through it as if through a magnifying glass.

"Suzy?" said Tribb. "Was it you?"

"Egg yolk," said Suzy. She looked up at Tribb, still squinting. "There's a tiny bit of egg yolk on this fork. At least I think it's egg yolk." She smiled. "It might be alien poo."

Tribb sighed. "None of the women in this house listen to me."

"Suzy," said Linda, still standing at the counter. "Did you take a bite out of these slices of bread and then put them back in the bag?"

Beside Tribb, Suzy made her scrunched-up, you-must-be-crazy face, with one eyebrow raised high. "Why the hell would I do *that*?"

"Suzy, don't swear," said Tribb. "Say heck instead of hell."

Suzy turned her you-must-be-crazy face to Tribb. "Why the *heck* would I do *that*?"

"Thank you."

Linda looked closely at the bread. "All these slices have a bite out of them in the same corner." She picked up the bag. "There's a hole in this bag."

She held it up so Tribb could see the hole. To Tribb, it looked about the size of his great-grandfather's thumb.

"I think we have mice," said Linda.

Chapter Three

Tribb was enjoying a beer with his friend Peter at the Cap and Cork Pub. They had met fifteen years before, when they both started working at Donner Metal Works. Tribb was a shift supervisor. No matter what day it was, he liked to arrive at work and joke, "Hope you enjoyed your weekend, boys. Munday's here already."

"You've been telling that joke for fifteen years and it still isn't funny," Peter would reply. "But keep trying."

Tribb always said that Peter was partly responsible for the life Tribb knew. About a year after they began working at Donner Metal Works, Peter had married a woman named Allison. Tribb was the best man at their wedding. At the wedding reception, Tribb had met Linda, who was a friend of Allison's. Linda was pretty, with long reddish-blond hair. "I liked your best man speech," she told Tribb at the reception. Then she rolled her eyes and grinned. "You tell terrible jokes."

Their life together had started that night. They dated for a while, and then they got married. Three years later, Suzy was born.

Whenever Peter had a problem in his life, he told Tribb about it, and they tried to work it out. The same was true for Tribb; if he had a problem, Peter was the first to know. They worked well together on problems because they had different ways of going at them. Tribb liked to look at things from all sides and think a lot before he acted. Peter would rather try right away to solve a problem with action.

Peter felt happiest when he could solve a problem by building something. He made stuff all the time in his garage workshop. Special holders for sharp knives and kitchen gadgets. Odd lamps to light a shelf or a cupboard. Bookcases with secret compartments. Once, Allison complained about having to lift the lid of the compost bin under the sink when her hands were full of kitchen scraps. So

Peter made a lever that would lift the lid every time Allison opened the cupboard door.

Peter's skill sometimes caused Tribb a bit of embarrassment. Tribb didn't feel very smart when it came to fixing things around the house. His father hadn't been much good at it, and so Tribb had never really learned. He could change a light bulb, of course. One time he'd changed a washer on a bathroom tap by looking at the pictures on the package. But that was about it.

So Tribb always dreaded going over to Allison and Peter's place for dinner. Every time, Allison had to show Linda the latest cool gadget Peter had made. When Allison pointed out how opening the cupboard door lifted the lid of the compost bin, Linda had been amazed.

"Why don't you make something like that for our house?" she asked Tribb.

Every time Linda wanted him to be more like Peter, Tribb could only shrug. "Peter's a builder," he'd say. "I'm a thinker."

Linda never seemed fully satisfied with this answer. In fact, lately, Tribb felt that Linda wasn't much satisfied with *him*. He knew husbands and wives sometimes went through stages when they weren't exactly thrilled with each other. He hoped they were just going through one of those times.

Anyway, when the two men were getting their beers in the pub, Tribb told Peter about his problem.

"We've got mice in our house."

And, of course, the first thing Peter said in reply was, "Great! I'll build you a mousetrap!"

Tribb waved him off. "I'm gonna handle this." He stared at his beer. "Mice," he muttered. "What is it they call mice? Vermin?" Tribb shuddered. Vermin was a word for pests that carried disease. Like the rats that caused the Plague in Europe hundreds of years ago, the disease that killed millions of people. In Tribb's mind, mice meant big, big trouble.

When Linda had shown him the bread bag with the hole in it that morning, she had been horrified. And then she had spent an extra long time cleaning the kitchen counters. He remembered her saying to him, "Mouse droppings are toxic. They make you sick. If they got into Suzy's food, I'd never forgive myself."

The look she gave him had made him feel pretty bad. Tribb thought it said, *And I'd never forgive you, either.* It was as if having mice in the house was *his* fault.

Now Tribb took a gulp of his beer. "I guess I have to buy some mousetraps," he said.

"What kind?" said Peter.

"I don't know," said Tribb. "I'll have to go to the store and see what they've got. Maybe just some of those regular wood traps. They work."

Peter shook his head. "That's old technology," he said. "They've got plenty of new ones now." He took a sip of his beer. "Why don't you just let me build one for you?"

Tribb sighed. "I'll think about it."

Peter looked at him and lifted his glass. "Buddy," he said, "you think too much."

On his way home from the pub, Tribb stopped at Home Depot. He had no idea where to find the mousetraps, and he felt too embarrassed to ask a clerk. Telling Peter about his mouse problem was one thing. Telling a stranger was different. The more Tribb thought about the problem, the more embarrassed he felt. Having mice in his home, he thought, said something bad about him.

Linda had asked him to hire a pest company to deal with the mice. But Tribb had refused. He didn't want a pest control truck parked in front of their house for all the neighbours to see. Whenever he saw one of those trucks in front of someone's house, he couldn't help himself. He thought that the people in that house must not keep it very clean. He always felt a little smug, a little better than those people. What kind of people let their house become infested?

Infested: such an ugly word. Words like that always seemed to have a bad story behind them. (*Divorce* was another one.) Tribb had lived his life without thinking *infested* would ever have anything to do with him. And now it did.

Tribb wandered through Home Depot looking for mousetraps. He figured the section would be small. It would be hidden away, like something shameful, next to the products for killing cockroaches. He wandered through the back part of the store, past the plumbing and lumber supplies, but had no luck. He finally worked up the courage to ask a sales person if she could direct him to the mousetraps. He had to force himself not to look at the floor when he asked her.

"Right up near the front," she said. "Aisle number two." Tribb noticed that the woman smiled as she said it. And the smile didn't seem sly or nasty. The woman didn't seem disgusted. In fact, she seemed quite cheerful, as if she pointed the way to the mousetraps every day. As if people came up to her all the time asking for directions to the mousetraps. As if it was no big deal.

The sales person's attitude made him feel a tiny bit better.

When he found the right section, Tribb was amazed. It was huge! He could see more than a dozen different ways to trap or kill mice. There were the regular snap traps made of wood, of course. There were also different kinds of plastic traps. Some looked like big plastic clothespins, others like plastic monster jaws. One gadget looked like some kind of mouse launching pad that would bounce the mouse off the ceiling. But Tribb knew that probably wasn't how it really worked.

Tribb also saw new "humane" traps that kept the mice alive. Why would you want to do that? Tribb wondered. The shelves of traps also had three or four kinds of mouse "repellers." They used sound to scare the mice out of the house. To Tribb, they looked like little stereo speakers. There were also pads the size of thin books, which promised to catch the mice with something sticky. And there was poison. Poison blocks. Poison pellets. Plenty of poison.

Tribb stared at all of these choices for a few minutes. He thought, Boy, a lot of people out there must have mouse trouble. An old saying came to mind: "Build a better mousetrap, and the world will beat a path to your door." At last he understood it. So many people had mice to get rid of that anyone who built the perfect mousetrap could get rich.

Clearly, a lot of companies were trying to do just that.

Tribb thought about Linda. How she had asked him to hire a company to solve the mouse problem. She must have decided he wouldn't be able to do the job properly himself. He badly wanted to prove her wrong. He badly wanted to show that he was clever, handy around the house, a reliable husband. Just like Peter.

Which trap should he get? The more Tribb looked at all the different kinds, the more confused he got. The more he thought about making a choice, the more he worried about making the *wrong* choice. The only ones that looked familiar were the old-style wooden snap traps. They were simple. They were tried and true. But Peter was right, they were old technology. Next to all the shiny new ideas, they seemed lame.

Tribb took a breath. Tried to relax. He looked around and saw the sticky pads. Something in him said *yes*. He thought back to that moment he saw something in the hall. That must have been a mouse scurrying along the floor. He'd lay some of these pads down, and the next time, that mouse would run right into trouble.

The pads were a lot more expensive than the old traps. That was another reason Tribb figured they had to be good. He bought three packages. Six pads in all.

Chapter Four

"What are those?" Linda asked.

It was the next morning, and Tribb had laid out six sticky mouse-catching pads. They were like plastic trays filled with glue. He had put three of the trays along the hall where he'd seen the mouse. After that, he'd set down three in the kitchen, near the stove, the fridge, and the sink. The glue was a soft, sweet-smelling gel, and very sticky to the touch. Tribb knew how sticky because he had touched the tip of one finger to it, just to test it. He'd had to pull very hard to get his finger loose. Actually, he felt a little frightened by how hard he'd had to pull.

"They're mousetraps," said Tribb proudly. "I got them last night."

"They don't look like mousetraps," said Linda. The way his wife was looking at the trays, Tribb could tell she wasn't sure they'd work. She picked one of them up to study it more closely. Tribb secretly wished she would touch a fingertip to the gel.

"They're the latest thing," said Tribb. "The mouse runs along the floor and sticks in the glue."

Linda lifted an eyebrow. "The mice have all this floor space to get where they're going. Why would they step into a tray like this?" She shook her head. "The mice will just run around it."

Tribb was starting to doubt the whole plan himself. But he couldn't let Linda see his doubt. "Maybe I'll put some cheese in the middle," he said. "They'll work. You'll see."

Linda just looked at him.

"If you want to see how sticky that gel is," said Tribb, "you could touch it with your finger."

"I think that would be a dumb thing to do," said Linda. "It's probably toxic."

Tribb looked at his own fingertip as Linda put the tray back down on the floor. She put her hands on her hips and looked around at the other trays Tribb had set out. "They don't look very nice," she said. She was right. They were ugly and black. "How long do they have to be here?"

Tribb shrugged. "Not long," he said. He heard Linda sigh.

"I've invited some people over for lunch on Thursday," she said. "All six of the moms in the school fund-raising group."

"This Thursday?" asked Tribb.

"Next Thursday," said Linda. "It's the only day that week I don't have to work at the hospital." She looked again at the sticky pads. "I want these to be gone by then."

That gave Tribb eight days. He didn't know how long it would take to get rid of the mice. But he did know he couldn't admit that to Linda. "I understand," he said. "No problem."

Linda took a deep breath, as if things were settled for now. "I still think you should have hired an expert to deal with this," she said.

A few minutes later, Suzy came down for breakfast. When she entered the kitchen she stopped dead in her tracks and pointed. "What are those, mouse swimming pools?" she asked. And Tribb had to go through the whole explanation again.

At work that day, Tribb told Peter about the sticky pads he'd bought to catch the mice. Peter just stared at Tribb.

"Sticky pads?" he said. "I could build you a custom, sure-fire mousetrap, but you thought it'd be better to buy sticky pads." Then Peter shook his head, as if Tribb had made a terrible mistake.

Everyone doubted him, thought Tribb. His best friend, his wife. Nobody believed he'd made the right choice. Well, never mind. *Somebody* had to feel good about things, so *he* would.

As the day went on, Tribb began to feel better. Even excited. Nobody had helped him find the pads, he'd found them on his own. He thought about them doing their job all day while he was at work. He couldn't stop imagining mice running along the floor and onto the sticky pads and getting stuck. The whole thing ran in his mind like a cartoon. As Tribb daydreamed about the mice getting stuck, he almost heard music. Fast music that suddenly stopped with a *sproing!* when the mice hit the gel. Sure, the idea was silly, but whenever he heard that *sproing!* in his head, he smiled. How satisfied he would feel, he thought, when he solved this mouse problem on his own. He didn't need help from any expert. Or Peter.

On the way home from work, Tribb's heart started to race. He had put a small chunk of cheddar cheese in the middle of each of the pads. That was sure to make them more effective. He figured there was a good chance he'd find a mouse on each one of his pads. Six pads, six mice. That would have to be all of them. Wouldn't it? He couldn't imagine that more than six mice were hiding in his house.

Tribb tried not to think about the fact that the mice would still be alive. That he would find the little mice there, wiggling and struggling to get free from the gel. Thinking about this made him think about Suzy. Little girls loved cute, furry animals. She wouldn't care that they were *vermin*. She'd just hate to see the mice trapped and struggling. Tribb knew that he would have to hide the pads and mice before Suzy found them.

Luckily, Suzy was supposed to be coming home late from school. Suzy played the trumpet in the school band, and every Wednesday she had band practice. Tribb checked his watch as he pulled in the driveway: five-thirty. He wasn't worried.

Tribb went in the back door, which was closest to the kitchen, ready for the sight of stuck mice. The first thing he saw was Suzy, sitting at the kitchen table.

"I thought you had band practice," said Tribb.

"Not this week," said Suzy. "The music teacher's sick."

"Huh," said Tribb. "Okay, then."

He took off his shoes, trying to act casual. Suzy seemed to be busy doing something. Tribb hoped she hadn't noticed the struggling mice that, he felt sure, were all around her. He didn't want to draw her attention to them.

He slowly looked down toward the pad he'd placed by the fridge. It was empty. That was a bit surprising. Tribb had figured the fridge pad would be the first one to grab a mouse. He looked next at the pad by the stove. Also empty. Tribb could feel his excitement fade. He looked for the third pad, the one he'd placed in the corner.

The pad was missing.

Then Tribb noticed what Suzy was doing as she sat at the kitchen table. She was tossing rolled up bits of paper at the wall. But what she was aiming for really got his attention. She had taped one of the mouse pads against the wall like a dart board. She was tossing the paper bits at the pad, trying to get them to stick!

"What the heck are you doing?" said Tribb. "That's for catching mice!"

"But this is fun!" said Suzy. "I'm really good at it."

The pad already had about six bits of paper stuck in the gel. It looked like Tribb's face after he shaved. After he stuck bits of toilet paper to the cuts to stop the bleeding. In the middle of the mouse pad was Tribb's piece of cheese.

"That's the bull's-eye," said Suzy.

"Come on, quit it," said Tribb. He went over to the wall and took down Suzy's target.

"Aw, Dad!"

Tribb tried pulling the bits of paper off, but they wouldn't budge. He wished Linda were here to see how sticky the gel was. "This one's ruined," Tribb said, giving Suzy a stern glance.

He decided he needed a beer and walked over to the fridge. As he went to open the fridge door, his sock foot landed smack on the sticky pad.

"Daddy!" said Suzy, as Tribb hopped around the kitchen. "You shouldn't swear!"

Chapter Five

Tribb still had four sticky pads, and he gave them a couple of days to catch something. All they caught, however, was dust and a bit of pasta. It was a noodle that flew out of the pot when Linda was stirring too hard as she made dinner.

"Cool," Suzy had said. "Do it again, Mom!"

On the third day, Tribb dumped the useless sticky pads into the garbage.

"I told you," said his friend Peter.

"What's the next plan?" asked Linda.

Tribb went back to Home Depot. He wasn't as self-conscious this time, didn't think people were staring at him. Just another ordinary customer with a mouse problem, that's all he was. He stood in front of the mousetrap display and considered his choices. He remembered something Suzy had said: "What happens to the mice when you catch them, Dad?"

Tribb realized she thought he was *catching* the mice, not *killing* them. He didn't want to upset her. So after a couple of minutes, he decided on the humane traps. They were like little square tubes with a hidden door that swung closed when a mouse came inside. Tribb didn't have a clue what he would do with a live trapped mouse. He just hoped he'd know when the time came. He bought five humane traps.

At home, Tribb took the traps out of their plastic packaging. They were more flimsy than he'd expected. Once he figured out how to set them, he needed some bait. In the fridge, he found some cheese wrapped in pink paper. The cheese looked different from the kind Linda normally got, and it was a bit smelly. Tribb thought the smell would probably make it good bait. He cut some small chunks off and placed them deep inside the traps. Then he cut some for himself, just to taste.

It was *good*. Rich and smoky. Tribb had never tasted cheese so yummy. He thought he'd ask

Linda to buy some more, but then he looked at the label. This cheese cost three times as much as the cheddar they usually ate. So this was a one-time treat! Tribb cut a few more slices for himself. He reached up for a new box of crackers he found in the cupboard. Were those mouse droppings on the shelf? He didn't want to know. He put the crackers and cheese onto a small plate. Then he set the traps around the kitchen.

Linda came home from her nursing shift at the hospital about an hour later. Not long after that, Tribb heard her shout from the kitchen, *"Who got into my cheese?"*

Tribb stepped into the bright light of the kitchen. He licked a crumb from the corner of his mouth and tried to explain. He told Linda about the new traps and how he'd needed cheese for the bait. He tried to make his eyes go wide with innocence. That trick had worked for Suzy when she got into the chocolate chips.

The look on Linda's face told Tribb that it didn't work for him. His wife was angry. "You needed *half* that cheese for the traps?"

"I tried a little bit, too," said Tribb.

"A little?" said Linda.

"More than a little," said Tribb. "It was *good*," he added, in case praise would help.

Linda crossed her arms and huffed. "That was special cheese, Tribb. I bought it for when the school sale group comes over next Thursday." Tears filled her eyes. She glanced at the cupboard. "I suppose you got into the special crackers, too?"

Tribb thought it best to say nothing. Linda looked terribly hurt; he didn't want to make things worse.

After a few seconds of looking at him, judging him, his wife shook her head and left the room.

Days went by, and no mice turned up in the traps. Linda kept finding mouse droppings around the food in the kitchen. She found even more in the cupboard under the sink. During breakfast, she would report her findings to Tribb. Then she cleaned the kitchen like a storm while he was trying to drink his coffee. He felt so bad about his wife working so hard, he offered to clean the kitchen himself. At this, Linda only made a snorting sound as she scrubbed.

There was one other reason for Linda's unhappiness. Her knitting was going slowly. Tribb thought he knew why.

At night, the family watched TV in the living room. Suzy would have her eyes on the show, and Tribb would watch Linda. As she worked on her knitting, she would shake out her left hand as if it hurt. She'd been going at it so long, Tribb figured, she was getting a strain injury. He sometimes saw injuries of that kind at the factory where he worked.

"You still have a lot of knitting to do?" asked Tribb.

"Mmm." Linda's needles clicked through a purple hat.

"Does your hand hurt?" Tribb asked. "Is there anything I can do?"

Linda looked sharply at Tribb. "How's the mouse problem coming?"

"Working on it," said Tribb. "Have to give it time."

"How much time?" Linda asked.

"Not much longer."

"Well, I'm glad you want to do something helpful," said Linda. Her voice was light, but she seemed to be speaking with a stiff jaw. "And I think getting rid of the mice would be wonderful."

"You guys are missing a great TV show," Suzy said.

That night, after Linda and Suzy were in bed, Tribb stayed up by himself, quietly watching the late news. He sat still in his chair for half an hour. He was trying not to think about anything. Not the cheese disaster. Not the sight of his wife shaking out her sore hand. Definitely not the fact that the one thing his wife wanted him to do, he wasn't doing.

Then something in the hall caught his attention. Without moving in his chair, he turned his eyes toward the hall. There was a mouse, a big one, making its way to the kitchen. A mouse! Right there! Tribb pressed back into his chair in horror. He held his breath. The mouse was about the length of his finger. To Tribb, it might as well have been a rat. There was no doubt now that his house was infested. This was proof!

Tribb knew he had to do something.

Within his reach, on a nearby bookshelf, sat a tall brass candlestick. Tribb imagined using it to club the mouse to death. As good as that would feel, however, it seemed too drastic. Tribb also figured he had only a slim chance of hitting the mouse in one try before it scooted away. Worse, if he *did* hit it, he would have a horrible mess to clean up. Forget the clubbing.

What he needed to do was catch the mouse! Time was running out. He looked around the living room for some kind of container. On the small table by the couch sat the antique crystal candy dish from Linda's grandmother. Tribb knew he couldn't use that, so he kept looking around. But there was nothing else, and the mouse was getting away!

Tribb rose from his chair, slowly and with the greatest care. He reached across to the side table and picked up the crystal candy dish. As quietly as possible, he dumped the candy from it onto the couch. Wrapped butterscotches slid into the cracks between the cushions.

The mouse was just about into the kitchen. It had a few inches of hallway carpet to go before it got to the shiny, hard tile. Tribb eased forward on his sock feet across the living room floor. He set each step down softly. It was how he used to leave Suzy's bedroom when she was a baby, finally asleep.

Light shone from the bright kitchen. Tribb could see the mouse scurrying toward that light. And the tile. Soon it would be too late. He held the dish high, like a hat he was about to put on. When he got to within a few steps of the mouse, he dove. He went head first, as if he was diving into a pool.

Right in the middle of diving for the mouse with the crystal dish, Tribb realized it was a bad idea. A terrible idea. Diving toward a creature so small and low was actually more like falling. He was *falling* toward the mouse. And as he was falling, he was trying to aim a crystal dish! Trying to aim it at a tiny thing that zigged and zagged, this way and that! For a second, Tribb was sure he had the mouse right where he wanted it, and then he didn't. The second was over, the mouse was gone. And the crystal dish was heading down, down, down toward the hard, bright tile.

The sound of the smash was almost musical. First came a single, high-pitched note as the dish hit the floor. Then came small, tinkling notes, as the broken pieces of crystal flew across the tile. It ended with the sound of Tribb groaning.

Linda came racing down the stairs, startled out of sleep. Tribb could see her face from where he lay on the floor. She came to him, her eyes full of concern. That look soon changed to shock. Then to sadness.

She pointed at the piece of crystal that remained in Tribb's hand. "Was that …?" He could only nod.

"Oh, Tribb," she said, her hand to her cheek. "What have you done?"

Chapter Six

Tribb hardly slept that night. Linda lay beside him in bed, with her back to him. She wouldn't respond when he kept saying "Sorry," over and over. He couldn't remember another time when his wife had been so upset, and he felt horrible. Tribb kept seeing Linda's face in his mind, her eyes filled with tears.

Maybe he was thinking too much, but he seemed to be stuck on a bad path. He wanted to make his wife feel better. Instead, he did things to make her feel worse. Tribb worried that if he didn't get off that path soon, Linda might just get fed up. And then what?

The next morning, while Linda and Suzy slept in, Tribb made himself coffee. He sat at the kitchen table and thought about what to do. Before his wife and daughter came downstairs, he got in the car and drove to Home Depot. One or two clerks nodded at him; he seemed to be a regular customer. Tribb charged past them, filled with purpose.

No more playing around with new ideas in mousetraps. He was getting the old-fashioned kind. The tried-and-true kind. He was buying wood-and-wire traps. They worked a hundred years ago, Tribb said to himself, and they'll work today!

When he got to the mousetrap section of the store, he looked down to the bottom. The last time he'd been to the store, he'd seen at least fifty wooden snap traps hanging there.

The traps were gone.

Tribb stared at the empty spaces in the display as if his eyes were playing a trick on him. As if all he had to do was wait, and the packages would appear, like magic. But they didn't.

Only one small package, with two little traps, hung from a wire arm. The rest of the spaces, where big packages of wood traps had hung, were empty. Tribb looked around the mousetrap section, trying to be hopeful. Maybe someone had moved the traps. But no. He could have as many new plastic traps as he wanted. He could load his arms up with sticky pads and poison if he cared to. But simple, honest, tried-and-true wooden traps? He was out of luck.

Tribb was starting to think the world was against him. Despair washed over him. He was about to close his eyes and let out a roar of frustration. Then another customer came around the corner. Tribb snapped out of his mood. He grabbed the last pack of wooden traps before it was too late.

Two middle-aged women in orange shirts stood behind the customer service counter. One of the ladies had a name badge that said "Carol." She wore glasses and had her straight brown hair tucked behind her ears. The other lady wore a badge with the name "Joan." She seemed older and had curly hair, dyed blond. Joan also wore bright red lipstick. This was a woman who cared about her looks, thought Tribb. He wondered if he should say something nice to her. Maybe the store kept some of the traps that he needed in the back, saved for special customers. Maybe if he paid Joan a compliment she would give him some.

Tribb held up the package in his hand for the woman to see, and he smiled at her.

"You look nice today," he said.

Joan looked up sharply at Tribb. He thought she frowned. "You sound surprised," she said. "Are you saying I don't look nice other days?"

Tribb took a half step away from the counter, as if it was hot. "No, oh no. I'm not saying that at all. I don't know what you look like other days."

"I look like this," said Joan. She glanced over at Carol and back at Tribb. She seemed hurt. Tribb tried to figure out how he had upset the woman by giving her a compliment.

"She *always* looks nice," said dark-haired Carol. She seemed confused, as if she wondered why Tribb would say such a *strange thing*.

"And why'd you just say that to *me*," said Joan. She pointed to the dark-haired woman. "Doesn't Carol look nice, too?"

Tribb felt his face getting hot. "She looks all right," he said.

"All right?" said Carol.

Tribb wished he were anywhere else but at that counter. Anywhere. The North Pole in a blizzard—that would be a better place to be than this. He waved the package in his hand. "I'm just looking to buy some more of these traps," he said.

"Oh," said Carol, all huffy. "Now you want *service*."

"You can't be rude to people and expect service," said Joan. "Didn't your mother teach you that?"

Tribb just stared helplessly at the women.

Suddenly, Joan grinned. "We're just teasing you, hon."

"We're just joking!" said Carol. She now had a big smile on her face. "You looked like you could use a little fun in your life!" She turned to her co-worker. "I think we upset him," she said.

Joan leaned forward on the counter, as if she was concerned. "Did we upset you?"

"Well," said Tribb. "I was a bit confused."

"I *know*," said Joan. "That's how we entertain ourselves."

"It breaks up the day," said Carol.

"Now," said Joan as she straightened. "How can we help you?"

Tribb asked if the store had any more wooden snap traps. "Maybe in the back?" he suggested.

The women just shook their heads. There'd been a run on those traps. Everyone was buying them.

"It's that time of year," said Joan.

"We had some last week," said Carol. "You should have come in then."

"I did," said Tribb. "I thought the new traps would be better."

Carol gave him a sad look. "That's what you thought, eh?" she said.

The two women glanced at each other, then back at Tribb.

"Do you do a lot of this sort of thinking?" asked Joan.

Tribb sighed. "Too much."

Chapter Seven

Tribb drove around for an hour looking for wooden traps, but every store was sold out of them. When he got home with his little pack of two, Linda and Suzy were gone. For a moment he thought the worst. Then he remembered it was Sunday. The two of them were probably swimming at the indoor pool at the community centre. Linda liked to swim on her days off, to relieve the stress of her nursing job.

Tribb thought back to when he and Linda first got married. Sometimes they went swimming together. In those days, Linda looked so beautiful in her swim suit, the sight of her made Tribb grin. Then, after Suzy was born, swimming was just a thing they did as parents. It was a way to entertain their toddler and get her tired enough to sleep through the night. Tribb figured that's when he stopped noticing how Linda looked in her swim suit. Not because she didn't look good, but because he was a dad now. He thought he should be paying attention to other things.

Here and now, in the kitchen, Tribb started to think that maybe he'd made a mistake. Something told him he'd been dumb not to enjoy seeing his wife in a swim suit. It was important in a way he couldn't quite name.

Tribb ripped open the plastic packaging and took out the wood snap traps. Now this was how a mousetrap should look. Everything about the design said, "You know me. I work." The wood base. The striker bar that you had to pull back. The wire hold-down rod that went over the bar. The catch that kept the bar in place. The little trigger plate that held the bait.

Setting up the traps was tricky. Tribb played with the first trap to get familiar with it. The catch was what they called a "hair trigger." The slightest pressure from the mouse on the bait plate would release the catch. That would release the hold-down rod. Then the striker bar would slam down.

The blow would break the mouse's neck. So the moment when you connected the hold-down rod to the bait plate was very…very…touchy.

"Shit!" shouted Tribb. The striker bar had slammed down onto his middle finger. The knuckle was red and throbbing. He sucked on his finger for a second and waved his hand in the air. Then he turned his attention to the bait.

He wasn't going anywhere near the cheese, that much was certain. He wasn't even going to look in the cheese drawer. But what could he use instead? He called Peter.

"I hear mice like bacon," said Peter.

"We don't have any bacon," said Tribb. "And if we did, I wouldn't be giving any to the mice. Gee, we've got some tomato and lettuce, too. Maybe you'd like me to make them a nice BLT sandwich."

"What's got you so crabby?"

"Sorry," said Tribb. "I'm just on edge. Linda's mad at me, for good reason. I broke her grandma's candy dish. I don't stare at her in her swim suit anymore. I haven't solved this mouse problem yet. And my finger hurts!"

"I'm coming over," said Peter. "And I'm bringing beer."

Peter arrived with a six-pack of beer. He eyed the traps on the kitchen table. "So you got the old wood ones, huh?" He picked one up and shook his head as if Tribb had made a big mistake. Then he saw Tribb was watching him. He put the trap down and shrugged. "Okay, I see two. Where are the others?"

"I only got the two," said Tribb. Peter looked at him and nodded for a while. Tribb just waited for what was going to come next. Finally, Peter stopped nodding.

"You think two's enough?"

"No, I *don't* think two's enough!" yelled Tribb. "They're all the store had left. There has been a *run* on these traps. *Everybody* is buying them! I should have bought a bunch of them when I had the chance. Instead of listening to you."

Peter put his hands up. "Hey, I didn't say don't buy them."

"You said they were old technology," said Tribb. "I was in the store and I heard your voice in my head: *old technology.* So then I bought a bunch of stupid traps that didn't work, and now my marriage is in trouble."

"*What?*" said Peter. "Your *marriage*?"

Tribb took a deep breath. "I'm probably making too much of things. It's just been a stressful few days. Linda's mad at me. I didn't get any sleep. She has all this knitting to do still. People are coming over, and I wasn't supposed to eat the cheese. And the women at the store were very confusing."

"*You're* confusing," said Peter. "I have no idea what you're talking about. What did you mean on the phone, about not staring at Linda in her swim suit?"

Tribb sighed and shook his head. "You ever think you might be taking your wife for granted?"

Peter wrinkled his forehead. "I don't know," he said. "I never thought about it."

"Yeah," said Tribb. "That's the difference between you and me."

The two men just stood quietly. Tribb looked at the floor with his hands on his hips. "You know, when you're married," said Tribb, "you have to worry about more than yourself. You have to worry about what someone else wants, all the time."

"Oh, like, she wants you to think she looks nice in a swim suit," said Peter.

"Yeah," said Tribb.

"And she wants you to get rid of the damn mice."

"Yeah," said Tribb. "And if you don't, you have a house with mice *and* an unhappy wife."

Peter reached into his six-pack, pulled out two beers, and handed one to Tribb. The two friends drank in silence for a few minutes, staring at the wood mousetraps.

"Marriage is hard," said Peter.

Tribb let out a deep breath. "Yeah," he said, and took a gulp of beer.

A minute later, Tribb said, "Now I need to figure out what to use for bait."

"And you won't use bacon," said Peter.

"No."

Peter put his hand to his chin for a moment. "I heard once that mice like dried fruit."

Tribb told Peter that he hated dried fruit. As far as he knew, they had none.

Peter snapped his fingers. "Chocolate!" he said. "Mice like chocolate."

"So does Linda," said Tribb. "She's already stopped speaking to me. I'm not using her chocolate."

Peter rubbed his chin some more. He stared at the kitchen cupboards, as if he was trying to imagine what was inside them. Then his eyes opened wide. "I know," he said. "Peanut butter!"

"Really?" said Tribb.

"Trust me," said Peter.

Tribb gave him a sideways look. "Aren't you the guy who talked me out of getting wood traps?"

"I said they're old technology," said Peter, and he grinned. "So's peanut butter."

For the next few minutes, Tribb and Peter worked with the two mousetraps. They looked like soldiers setting bombs in a war zone. They put peanut butter on each bait plate, then carefully set the striker bars. After a few mistakes and cries of pain, they were ready. Tribb laid the two baited traps carefully in the hallway, against the wall.

"That's where I keep seeing the mice," he said. "Might as well try there first."

After that was done, the two men sat back down at the kitchen table. They talked about work and opened two more beers. They hadn't taken more than a few sips when they heard a loud *snap!* from the hallway. Tribb and Peter looked at each other for a moment, frozen. They knew what had just happened.

"It hasn't even been five minutes!" said Tribb.

Slowly the two men got up from the kitchen table and started toward the hall. Tribb went first, nervously, his heart beating hard. He peered around the frame of the doorway, into the hall.

And there it was.

A grey mouse about the size of his whole thumb lay caught in the first trap they'd put down. It had gone for the peanut butter, and the striker bar had slammed down onto the mouse's back. But when he and Peter stood over the mouse and stared down, Tribb was horrified.

"It's not dead," said Tribb, almost in a whisper.

"I know," said Peter.

"It's still *moving*!" said Tribb.

"I *know*," said Peter.

For a moment they watched the mouse in the trap, not believing what they were seeing. The mouse was pinned and flattened, but its furry back legs were still wiggling. It kept on trying to get free. The sight was awful.

"Goddamn it," said Tribb. "That thing is *suffering*. What do we do?"

"You have to kill it," said Peter.

"What?" exclaimed Tribb. "I can't kill anything. That's what the frigging trap is supposed to do!"

"Calm down," said Peter.

Tribb started to breathe hard. Part of him worried that somehow the mouse might actually wiggle free and get away. Another part thought about Linda and Suzy coming home. They could walk in at any minute, and Tribb couldn't bear to let his daughter see this.

"I guess you could just throw it into the garbage," said Peter.

"Just throw it into the garbage and let it die slowly?" said Tribb.

Peter shrugged. "It's only a mouse."

"I can't do that."

"Or you could drown it," said Peter.

Tribb imagined filling a sink with water and holding the wounded mouse under the surface until it stopped moving. He knew that was how they used to kill unwanted kittens on farms. He pictured himself washing dishes later in the same sink and shuddered.

Then Tribb tried thinking about how things die naturally, in the wild, and an idea came to him.

Every winter the news would report that someone had frozen to death in a blizzard. Those reports always said the same thing. They said that after a while, in extreme cold, you begin to feel warm. After that you just ... fall asleep, never to wake up.

If he had to kill something, Tribb thought, making it fall asleep seemed the nicest way to do it. He took a deep breath.

"We'll freeze it," he said.

"Freeze it?" said Peter. "How?"

"How do you freeze anything? Put it in the freezer." He began to look around the kitchen. "Just have to find something to put it in."

At that moment, he heard the sound of a car pulling into the driveway.

"That's Linda and Suzy!" said Tribb. "Quick, find a container!" He began to bang cupboard doors open, searching.

"What?" said Peter. "You mean, like, a box?"

"Not a box!" said Tribb. "It has to fit into the freezer." He pointed to the top of the fridge.

Peter looked from the fridge to Tribb. He seemed shocked. "You mean you don't have a big storage freezer in the basement?"

Tribb dropped down to his hands and knees to look in the cupboards under the counter. "Linda always says we should get one, but I've never thought we needed it." Another way he had failed his wife, and now it was coming back to haunt him. "Crap! I thought there were old plastic yogurt tubs under here!"

He heard the car doors shut outside — *chunk, chunk*. He heard the voices of Linda and Suzy as they walked toward the back door. The mouse was still pinned in the trap. Still wiggling. All Tribb could find was a see-through Tupperware container. Would that do?

"Got it!" said Peter.

Tribb saw Peter holding an empty cookie tin. The kind that held the special shortbreads Linda loved.

"Perfect!" said Tribb. "Where'd you find it?"

"Uh," said Peter.

Tribb didn't wait for an answer. He grabbed the tin and dumped in the mousetrap with the wiggling mouse. As he fit the lid over the tin, Tribb could see the mouse kicking desperately. Then he opened the freezer and shoved in the tin. In with the frozen hamburger, peas, toaster waffles, and Popsicles.

The back door opened. Tribb tried to calm his breathing as he turned to greet his wife and daughter. At the same time, Peter came up beside him with his hands behind his back. Tribb felt Peter nudge him with his elbow. He seemed to want to give Tribb something without anyone seeing.

"Hi, girls!" said Tribb brightly, as if he hadn't just shoved a live animal into their freezer. Secretly, Peter passed him a plastic bag filled with shortbread cookies.

Chapter Eight

Catching one little mouse was a small thing, Tribb knew, but still he felt good. He'd done something right. After Peter headed home and Suzy went upstairs to change, Tribb told Linda proudly, "I got a mouse!"

Linda gave him a small smile. She didn't seem as thrilled about the mouse as he'd hoped. Tribb felt a little disappointed. He thought maybe he needed to tell her a bit more.

"Big one, too," he said. Tribb held his fingers wide to show the mouse's length and puffed out his chest with pride. Then he started to point to the refrigerator.

"Just so you know, it's —"

Linda stopped him. "I don't need to know the details, Tribb. I just need to know you're handling this. I've got so much work to do still, and I'm going to have a kitchen full of guests in four days."

"Right."

He watched Linda go into the living room. She was already getting to work on another batch of scarves and hats for the school. It was hard for Tribb to see his wife like this, tired and frustrated. He was annoyed with her for taking on the extra work. He was annoyed with himself for not being able to make life easier for her.

"Hey," he said. He walked past the one remaining mousetrap in the hall and followed Linda into the living room. "Let me help you with that knitting."

Linda was setting herself up on the couch. Golden afternoon light shone through the big picture window. Linda's cloth knitting bag lay over on its side on the floor. She turned it upright, then lifted out her needles and a grey hat she'd almost finished.

"Tribb, there's nothing you can do to help me," Linda said with a sigh. "Except maybe make me a cup of tea."

Within a few minutes, Tribb had made a steaming cup of Linda's favourite raspberry tea. He set it on a wooden coaster beside her, the way she liked. She thanked him and smiled as she brought it to her lips. Her smile made Tribb feel warmer than he had in days. Then he set himself down on the couch beside her.

"So I want to help you knit," Tribb said. "Maybe I could hold the yarn or something. I've seen people do it in movies."

Linda made a *pffft* sound and shook her head. "You'll be bored to death," she said. "You won't last five minutes."

"Sure I will!" Tribb gave his wife a big smile, to show his good intentions. He saw the line of grey yarn that stretched from his wife's needles to the knitting bag. He reached into the bag and pulled out the fuzzy ball of yarn. A few of the other yarn balls, some grey, some green, rolled and adjusted to the new space.

"What do I do?" Tribb asked.

Linda paused, then said, "Just keep turning the ball so the yarn falls off the bottom. Let it hang loose." A small smile crept onto her face. "Thank you."

For a few minutes, the two of them sat like that. Tribb kept turning the ball so the yarn hung down, and Linda knitted happily. And they just talked. They chatted about Suzy, about her school marks, about her swimming. Linda told him what was going on at the hospital. Tribb learned about problems she was having with a young nurse who didn't listen. He learned about doctors who were good to work with and some who were rude. He was amazed at all the romances going on between the younger doctors and nurses.

Tribb enjoyed every minute, and he felt Linda did too. They were having their best time together in months. Tribb even remembered to tell his wife, "You look great in that sweater." And he was glad when she seemed pleased.

In the moments of happy silence, Tribb's mind wandered a little. He thought about how he'd taken the bag of shortbread cookies and shoved it into the cleaning closet. Linda wouldn't like that. Tribb wondered if he could get the cookies back into the tin without her finding out. He'd have to remember to wash it out first, after the mouse was fully frozen and dead.

Thinking about the mouse made Tribb remember that he had only one mousetrap left. He wondered if that was enough. Then he had a hopeful thought. Maybe there'd only ever been one mouse in the house. Maybe the problem was solved! Tribb relaxed a little. He liked the idea that his mouse troubles were over. He smiled at Linda. Maybe his marriage troubles were over, too.

At that moment, down in the cloth knitting bag by Tribb's feet, something moved. He caught the movement out of the corner of his eye and glanced down, not really worried. Maybe Linda had nudged the bag with her foot. Maybe the balls of yarn were just shifting again.

But no. That wasn't it.

As he looked down into the bag, he saw one of the small grey yarn balls jiggle. Just slightly. And then it disappeared.

When it reappeared, a few inches away from where it had disappeared, Tribb knew. It wasn't a small ball of yarn at all. And he took in a sharp breath.

"What, honey?" Linda asked. "Did you just remember something?"

Tribb looked up at his wife. Linda was focused on her needles, not looking at him. She didn't know he was reacting to something in her knitting bag. She was completely unaware. In a way, Tribb thought, he and Linda now lived in different times. He was living in the present, knowing the terrible truth about what was in her bag. But Linda was still in the past, before that truth had been discovered. He wished he could be back there with her, still unaware. Still happy.

Tribb wondered, could he just *not* tell her? Could he ignore what was going on in the bag at her feet? Could he drop the ball of yarn and pull his wife into his arms in a romantic rush? Could he tell her that he was taking her and Suzy out for dinner? Maybe he could. He wanted to. But then he asked himself another question. Could he enjoy that dinner, knowing what he knew?

No, he couldn't. This small, quiet moment of happiness was about to come to an end. There was no way out. He hated that he was so alert, that he could see so well out of the corner of his eye. This talent was ruining his life. He took a deep breath.

"Linda, honey," Tribb said. "I have something to tell you, and you're not going to like it."

Chapter Nine

Tribb was right about that: Linda didn't like what he had to tell her. At all.

The news that she had mice living in her knitting bag horrified her. Worst of all, she told Tribb, she would have to throw out all of the knitting she'd done. "Every hat," she'd said, crying. "Every scarf!"

"Why?" Tribb said. He thought about how many hours of work she'd put in, the pain in her hands. "Why throw it all out?"

"I'm a nurse," she said. "I know how disease spreads. I don't know which things have been touched by filthy mice. A child might put a dirty scarf against her face."

Tribb asked her why she couldn't just wash everything before selling it. Linda's face went red. She looked down and picked up a hat she'd made.

"This is the only creative thing I do," she said. "I'm proud of it. Nothing makes me happier than showing off the bright new things I've made. And if I have to wash everything first"—she stared straight at him—"it will all look *used*."

Linda threw her knitting bag, mice and all, and all the clothing items she'd made, into a garbage bag. She took the garbage bag straight out to the curb. She wouldn't let Tribb help her. The sadness in her face as she did this was heartbreaking. And Tribb felt that Linda's sadness went beyond her lost knitting. Beyond all the hours of wasted effort. She seemed to be sad about her whole life. Her life with him.

Then and there, Tribb decided to do what he should have done at the very beginning. At the very first sign of mouse trouble. He decided to call an expert.

Monday morning, after Linda left for the hospital and Suzy went to school, Tribb called Best Pest Control. Four hours later, the truck pulled up in front of the house. Tribb looked out the front window. He saw the truck, with its name in big letters, and sighed. What would the neighbours be saying? Then he slapped his forehead. That was that kind of thinking that had gotten him into trouble in the first place. When the doorbell rang, he opened the front door. There stood a tall man in a dark blue uniform.

"Mr. Munday?" said the man, glancing up from the clipboard in his hands. He grinned. "Don't worry sir, I like Mundays."

Tribb tried to smile but couldn't. "Come in," he said.

Together they walked through the main floor of the house. The Best Pest man said mice usually come into the basement from the outside. "When it starts getting cold in the fall," he said, "they head for warmth. Once they're inside, they head for the food, which is usually on the main floor." He pointed to the heating vent in the hallway. "That's probably one of the places they're coming up." Sure enough, Tribb had caught his one mouse right beside the vent.

In the kitchen, the pest man looked for holes in the wall near the refrigerator and the stove. He shone a bright flashlight into the cupboard under the sink. "They like to crawl up the outside of the pipes, too." He pointed to a gap between the pipe and the wall. "Right there," he said. "That's a mouse doorway."

The Best Pest man stood up. "I can place traps all over the main floor. They're small and black. I'll put them in corners so no one will notice them. They use poison bait, which the mice love. So do pets, though. Do you have pets?"

Tribb said no.

"We're good, then," said the Best Pest man. "The poison works fast. Most of the mice in a house usually die in a couple of days."

A couple of days would be great, thought Tribb. There was just enough time before Linda's group came for its meeting.

"But that's only part of your problem," said the Best Pest man. "You have to stop the mice getting in. Otherwise, you'll just keep getting new visitors." He snapped off his flashlight. "Let's have a look outside."

They started at the back door and walked all around the house. Every few steps, the Best Pest man stopped and pointed. A small hole in the foundation. A gap between the bricks. A space around the wood of a basement window. "They don't need much room," said the man. He held up his little finger. "If I can wiggle this finger into a space, that's big enough for a mouse."

"What do I do?" asked Tribb.

"Plug every hole. If it's in the foundation or the brick, patch it with fresh concrete. If it's in the wood, stuff the hole with copper wool. That'll keep 'em out. Mice don't like to bite down on copper wool."

Tribb knew he could get a tub of concrete filler from Home Depot, but he'd never seen copper wool. When he asked where he could buy it, the Best Pest man said he had some in the truck.

"It's just like steel wool," he said, "but it shines like a new penny. And it doesn't rust."

Tribb knew he needed to deal with this now. He called work and said he was too sick to come in. Within half an hour, the Best Pest man had placed his traps. He showed Tribb how to stuff holes with the copper wool. Then Tribb drove to the store and came home with a plastic pail of concrete filler.

Before he got started, the phone rang. It was Peter calling.

"I heard you're sick," Peter said. "Is that true?"

"I'm sick of mice and what they're doing to my life," said Tribb. "Today's the day I get rid of them for good."

Tribb worked for hours. He stuffed copper wool into twenty-three gaps. He patched every crack he could find in the brick and the foundation. The old house had a lot of holes. More holes than he could ever have imagined. This was a house shouting to the world of mice, "Come on in!" Tribb promised himself that he would patch every single tiny space. Even if all he could fit into it was a fingernail.

Halfway through the day, he ran out of concrete filler. He drove to the store to get some more. The sun set, and Tribb kept on patching. His hands turned raw from scrapes against the bricks and cramped from holding the trowel. When Linda came home from work, she sat in the car for a moment watching him. Then she got out and came to where Tribb was kneeling.

"What are you doing?" she asked. "Sealing the house," he said. "I hired an expert. He showed me how. Nothing's ever getting in to bother us again."

An hour and a half later, Linda came outside and told him dinner was ready.

"Keep it warm," he said. "I'll come in as soon as I'm finished."

A few minutes later, Suzy came outside, holding her arms tight in the cold. "Dad, aren't you hungry?" she asked.

He was, and his back was killing him, but he wasn't going to admit it. "Almost done," he said.

It was nearly nine o'clock when Tribb finally staggered into the house. He stood in the kitchen, dead tired. His hands were scraped. His face and his clothes were covered with dirt and bits of dried concrete.

"Wow, Dad," said Suzy. "You look like you were in a fight."

Linda looked over at him and smiled. "He was," she said. She came up to Tribb and took his dirty face in her hands. "Thank you for working so hard," she said, and laid a soft kiss on his lips.

"I did it for you," Tribb told her. "I don't want to lose you."

Linda looked into his eyes. "Lose me?" she said.

"I haven't been a great husband lately," he said.

She smiled a little. "No one's perfect," she said, and kissed him again.

The next two days, Tuesday and Wednesday, were two of the best days Tribb could remember. He felt pride in himself. He felt loved. His world was back on track. At work, he was a happy supervisor. He hummed as he went from station to station, slapping people on the back, telling bad jokes at lunch. At home, he was deeply contented. He helped Suzy with her homework. He bought a new knitting bag for Linda. He made dinner while she worked on her new hats and scarves and brought her cups of tea through the evening.

There were no more signs of mice.

Thursday came, Linda's day off. She spent the morning preparing for her group's visit at noon. Tribb arranged to work the late shift so he could stay home to help. When the six women arrived, he greeted them, shaking hands and welcoming them into his mouse-free home. He poured soft drinks for the guests. Then he kissed his wife on the cheek and said he'd be in the basement if she needed him.

Patching all the holes around the house had been hard work. But Tribb felt so satisfied doing it, he'd decided to take on other projects. The first thing he wanted to make was a wooden gadget to hold

Linda's balls of yarn. It would let them turn easily, like a roll of toilet paper. She'd be so surprised!

In the basement, Tribb could hear some of the things the women were saying in the kitchen above. One of the women said to Linda, "Your husband seems so helpful!"

"He's a real sweetheart," said another.

Tribb smiled as he heard Linda agree, and he knew that life could not get more perfect. For a while, as he worked on his project, he lost track of what they were saying upstairs. But now and then he heard the clink of plates or glasses as the women enjoyed their lunch.

About an hour later, Tribb noticed the sound of dishes being cleared in the room above. He heard Linda ask if anyone wanted a cup of coffee or tea. Tribb briefly wondered whether he should go up and help Linda, but he decided not to. His yarn holder was coming along, and he wanted to stick with it.

Still, something nagged at Tribb. He smelled the coffee brewing upstairs and felt there was something he needed to do. He knew it had to do with the lunch, and with Linda. It was something important. He just couldn't put his finger on what it was.

A minute later, Tribb heard Linda say the word "dessert." The women in the kitchen all made happy sounds, as if they thought dessert was a great idea. Downstairs in the basement, Tribb knocked his head with his fist, trying to remember what he needed to do.

Then, above him, Linda said something about her "favourite cookies," and Tribb stood straight up. He heard his wife say, in a voice of pure delight, "Oh, here they are! I wonder what they were doing in the freezer."

Tribb was flying up the stairs when he heard the screams.

Good Reads

Discover Canada's Bestselling Authors with Good Reads Books

Good Reads authors have a special talent—
the ability to tell a great story, using clear language.

Good Reads can be purchased as eBooks, downloadable
direct to your mobile phone, eReader or computer.
Some titles are also available as audio books.

To find out more, please visit
www.GoodReadsBooks.com

The Good Reads project is sponsored by
ABC Life Literacy Canada.

Grass Roots Press

Good Reads Series

Coyote's Song
by Gail Anderson-Dargatz

Sara used to be a back-up singer in a band. She left her singing career to raise a family. She is content with being a stay-at-home mom. Then, one Saturday, Sara's world changes.

Sara and her family go to an outdoor music festival. There, on stage, Sara sees Jim, the lead singer from her old band. He invites her to sing with him. Being on stage brings back forgotten feelings for Sara—and for Jim. And Sara's husband Rob sure doesn't like what he sees.

Sara also sees something else: a coyote. Learn how Coyote, the trickster spirit, turns Sara's life upside down.

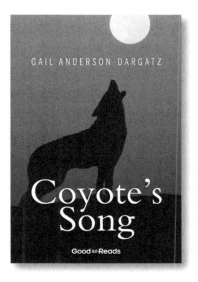

The Break-In
By Tish Cohen

Marcus and Alex have two things in common—they each have a broken heart and a plan.

Marcus wants to win back his girlfriend. He is ready to stage a break-in for her. Eleven-year-old Alex wants to find his father's killer. He has a gun and may be ready to use it.

When Marcus and Alex cross paths, they make a mess. But in a strange way, they also begin to understand each other. *The Break-In* is a funny story about finding brotherhood in dark times.

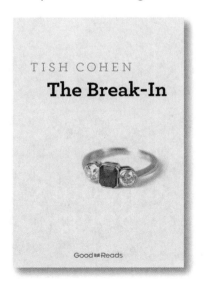

Listen!

By Frances Itani

Liz invites her sister, Roma, and two friends to dinner. The four women have something important in common: they are hearing daughters of deaf parents. Each woman brings an old family picture to the table. Each tells a story about her picture.

Roma has always felt alone and different. As a child, she had to "listen and tell." Roma became the listener because her mother could not hear. But by the end of the evening, Roma knows she is not alone. She and the other women learn that growing up with deaf parents has given them rare and special gifts.

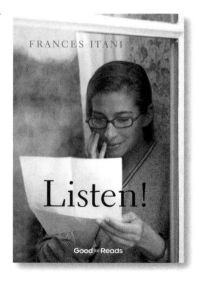

About the Author

 *The Globe and Mail* called Trevor Cole "one of the best young novelists in Canada." Trevor Cole has written three bestselling novels. His most recent, *Practical Jean*, won the 2011 Leacock Medal for Humour. Trevor has also won nine National Magazine Awards for his work as a journalist.

Also by Trevor Cole:

Norman Bray in the Performance of His Life
The Fearsome Particles
Practical Jean

You can visit Trevor's website at
www.trevorcole.com